Clip & Go!

FALCON®

CHOCKSTONE®

◆ HOW TO ROCK CLIMB SERIES ◆

Clip & Go!

tips and tricks for the modern sport climber

John Long
Duane Raleigh

illustrations by Mike Clelland

FALCON®

CHOCKSTONE®

HOW TO ROCK CLIMB: CLIP & GO!

© John Long and Duane Raleigh 1994. All rights reserved. Printed in the United States of America. No part of this book may be used or reproduced in any manner whatsoever without written permission of the publisher, except in the case of brief quotations embodied in critical articles and reviews.

1 2 3 4 5 6 7 8 9 0 VP 04 03 02 01 00

COVER PHOTO:

All uncredited photos by Duane Raleigh

Cataloging-in-Publication data is on record at the Library of Congress

ISBN 0-934641-84-6

PUBLISHED AND DISTRIBUTED BY:
Falcon Publishing, Inc.
P.O. Box 1718
Helena, MT 59624

OTHER BOOKS IN THIS SERIES:
Better Bouldering
Big Walls
Building Your Own Indoor Climbing Wall
Climbing Anchors
Clip and Go!
Flash Training!
Gym Climb
How to Climb 5.12!
How to Ice Climb!
How to Rock Climb!
I Hate to Train
Knots for Climbers
More Climbing Anchors
Nutrition for Climbers
Self-Rescue
Sport Climbing
Top-Roping

WARNING: CLIMBING IS A SPORT WHERE YOU MAY BE SERIOUSLY INJURED OR DIE

READ THIS BEFORE YOU USE THIS BOOK.

CLIP & GO!

JOHN LONG and
DUANE RALEIGH

This is an instruction book to rock climbing, a sport that is inherently dangerous. You should not depend solely on information gleaned from this book for your personal safety. Your climbing safety depends on your own judgment based on competent instruction, experience, and a realistic assessment of your climbing ability.

There is no substitute for personal instruction in rock climbing and climbing instruction is widely available. You should engage an instructor or guide to learn climbing safety techniques. If you misinterpret a concept expressed in this book, you may be killed or seriously injured as a result of the misunderstanding. Therefore, the information provided in this book should be used only to supplement competent personal instruction from a climbing instructor or guide. Even after you are proficient in climbing safely, occasional use of a climbing guide is a safe way to raise your climbing standard and learn advanced techniques.

There are no warranties, either expressed or implied, that this instruction book contains accurate and reliable information. There are no warranties as to fitness for a particular purpose or that this book is merchantable. Your use of this book indicates your assumption of the risk of death or serious injury as a result of climbing's risks and is an acknowledgement of your own sole responsibility for your climbing safety.

(photo opposite)

*Christian Griffith on the
Cloven Hoof, 5.13c,
Crystal River Valley,
Colorado.*

C O N T E N T S

CLIP & GO!

JOHN LONG and
DUANE RALEIGH

CHAPTER 1

INTRODUCTION

Perhaps a dozen years ago, steep, bolt-protected sport climbs swept through the climbing world like a gorilla monsoon. And the storm blows on, from France to Alabama, from Austria to Timbuktu. Loose from the chains of tradition, climbers focused on explosive, gymnastic movement and the pursuit of absolute difficulty continue to lace up, tie in, clip and go. This manual relates the tricks, strategies, techniques and specific equipment that top climbers use for the most demanding clip and go climbs. The moves are hard enough. Also having to second-guess the best way to go about your business puts you at a genuine, and needless, disadvantage. This manual is geared to eliminate second-guessing, and to free you to concentrate on the climbing.

The degree of difficulty between entry-level and world-class clip-and-go routes varies substantially, but the generic methods used to scale them are uniform because the medium is of a piece: bolt-protected face climbs. *Clip & Go!* is not a handbook on how to clasp holds or place your feet. For the low-down on the boundless topic of physical movement, check *Sport and Face Climbing!*, also in the *How to Rock Climb!* series.

Clip-and-go routes are not for beginners, nor is this manual. A clip-and-go route easier than 5.10b is the exception; and while 5.10b might seem casual enough in the gym, on an actual crag it marks the threshold into advanced turf. Only now are climbers beginning to understand that pumping plastic is not the identical twin of climbing on real rock. The two are more like second cousins. Many climbers accustomed to cranking 30 feet of 5.12 indoors have found themselves overwhelmed on, say, a minimal 5.11 pocket climb up a 120-foot, overhanging wall of welded tuff. In any event, this manual assumes you have a sound understanding of all the basic climbing procedures, and is principally aimed at refining your understanding by condensing and dishing up only the latest inside dope particular to clip-and-go routes.

We'll also take a close look at certain scenarios that continue to result in unnecessary injuries to sport climbers. The vast majority of clip-and-go routes are bolted top to bottom, and are located on small bluffs and outcrops. Generally, the approach is short, the weather good, and the routes short, and all this contributes to an arena and an activity that is far more contained and manageable than a 10 pitch adventure climb in the High Sierra. Yes, much of the jeopardy has been engineered out of clip-and-go routes; but no climb is without danger. All climbing is potentially fatal if basic safety procedures are not followed, and followed precisely. Since most sport climbs are for advanced climbers, it's the experts who

Christina Jackson on Pigs in Zen, 5.12a, Crystal River Valley, Colorado.

Duane Raleigh photo

have generally gotten hurt. Lynn Hill was lowering off a sport climb in France and came detached from her rope, slamming into the ground. Richard Harrison was being lowered from a clip-and-go route in Las Vegas when the belayer lost track of how much rope remained. Suddenly, the end of the rope whizzed through the belay device—and Richard plunged 30 feet to the deck. Greg Child was descending a sport climb in Washington and rapped off the end of his rope. These three climbers are very experienced, and all three had accidents that should have killed them. Many of us have. We'll take a look at how to avoid such accidents.

First, however, we will work through the gear.

EQUIPMENT:

CHAPTER 2

ROPES

Sport climbing is harsh medicine for ropes, much more so than traditional free climbing. In sport climbing, you often fall, yard back up the rope, then fall off again and again, before finally lowering off. And you may repeat this process dozens of times a day, generally on the same section of rope. Though the actual falls are often short and seemingly trivial, they add up fast and, combined with all the assorted frigging, greatly hasten rope wear. More so than longer falls, short falls on short sections of rope put more force on your line, your protection and yourself. This is because in any fall, the cord acts as a sort of spring, stretching to absorb the impact. The more rope out, the longer the spring. Given the standard eight- to 10-foot sport-climbing fall on a climb that is seldom longer than 80 feet, every fall is a wrencher. And the cord remembers the thrashing it has taken. A clip-and-go climber must factor all this into the equation when purchasing a rope.

Sport climbers should only climb on UIAA-certified single ropes. Double ropes are too confusing and unwieldy to work with. While some climbers—hoping to shave off ounces and gain an edge—may chose a single, skimpy, 9-mm line (or one of even smaller diameter), don't try this at home. Lone 9-mm ropes were not fashioned to withstand the forces and continual abuse that a clip-and-go route invariably places on them. So go with a stout, single rope in the 9.8- to 11-mm range. The 9.8-mm lines save a few ounces and are easier to clip, but a 10-foot fall will almost always have a greater impact on a thin rope than a thicker one; and the thinner ropes abrade much faster no matter their dynamic qualities. Ten-point-five- and 11-mm ropes yield softer catches, are easier on the belayer's hands and are generally more wear-resistant. If greenbacks allow, buy two ropes: a 9.8-mm for redpoint and flash attempts, and a 10.5- or 11-mm cord for "working" routes.

Modern sport routes usually have a bolted lowering station at the 80-foot mark, enabling you to lower off with a single 165-foot rope. With that in mind, make sure the rope you buy is at least 165 feet (50 meters) long—preferably longer. I (D.R.) use 180-foot (55 meter) ropes, just in case the person who bolted the route used a long rope and placed the lowering anchors to accommodate his extended cord.

BUY LINE

When buying a rope, a primary concern is its maximum impact force, listed in pounds or kilograms on the rope's hang tag. Compare the tags from several ropes. Lines with higher maximum impact forces will catch you harder than those with lower numbers; the latter are preferred for obvious reasons. Also, glance at the number of UIAA falls held (meaning the number of test falls the line will hold before it snaps), but don't place too much stock on super high numbers. A 15-fall rope sounds impressive, but in actual practice, it is no better than a 10-fall rope. Both cords will break in the lab, but not in the field, and the 15-fall rope is always far more costly.

No one sport climbs in the rain, but buy a rope with a "dry" coating nonetheless. Ropes with a water-repellent treatment are softer, less prone to kink, and slide more freely over the rock and through the biners. The dry coating also increases wear resistance and reduces the degenerative effects of sunlight—which can age a rope faster than any other cause, save abuse.

Treated ropes usually have a soft "hand," but ropes that are as limp as overcooked noodles are just as hard to work with as ones that are cable-stiff. Somewhere in between lies the ideal hand. Since you cannot tell how a rope will handle until you unflake it from its factory coil and climb on it for several days, buying your dream rope is a crapshoot. Most climbers burn through several brands before settling on the rope they most prefer. A last consideration is the sheath. Dirt has a hard time penetrating ropes with tight, smooth sheaths; these ropes also slip over the rock more fluidly than loosely woven or coarse-sheathed lines.

VESTAL ROPE

Your rope is your life. Take care of it. Never chuck your rope in the dirt, which acts as an abrasive and can adversely effect its manageability—even more than UV rays, which "cook" a rope over time, making it stiff. The ground at sport crags is often as filthy as a strip-joint ashtray, so as a matter of course, flake out your line onto a rope tarp. Any kind of tarp is better than nothing—those funky blue vinyl jobs from K-Mart work, but the specialized ones made by Black Diamond and Metolius are better. They roll up into neat packages, have a pocket or two in which you can stash stash loose items, and feature carrying straps. If anyone steps on your rope—spank him.

Keeping the rope clean eliminates the need to wash it, but should some bumbly soil your cord, put it in a tub of lukewarm water, add a mild soap (call the rope manufacturer to find out what is safe for the brand), and swish it around until it appears clean. Rinse and air dry. Do not put your rope in a washing machine or dryer. Both will ruin it.

Bird Lew on Heinous Cling, Smith Rock, Oregon.

Kevin Powell photo

RETIREMENT PLAN

Only you can determine when your rope is no longer safe. In general, retire a rope when it starts showing its use, usually when it has become "furry," or develops flat or soft spots. The 20 feet on each end of a rope always sees the most wear, as these sections saw back and forth through the high draws when you fall or work a route. When either end piece starts getting trashed, cut it off, and use the remaining short rope. But remember, this shorter rope may now look swank, but it has held just as many falls as the piece you cut off. Use it with discretion, and make certain it is still long enough to lower you off a route.

CORD CONVALESCENCE

After you fall, clip off or lower off the route, and let the rope rest for a few minutes before clawing back onto the rock to ping off again. Those couple of minutes will give the rope (and your heated tendons) time to recover some capacity to stretch and absorb force. Because the tie-in knot likewise absorbs energy when it cinches tight, make it a habit to untie, rest up, and tie back in each time you lower to the deck; or better yet, switch to the fresh end of the rope.

HARNESSES

Most manufacturers make a harness model specifically for sport climbing. Feather-light and stronger than you'll ever need, a minute after stepping into a first-rate harness it'll be hard to remember you have one on. A harness should be easy to put on and take off, comfortable, and not burdened with silly embroidery, vinyl or plastic ornaments, needless buckles and do-dads, or any pressure points that can abrade the sport climber like a burr under the saddle.

Key features include a strong belay loop and a sufficient number of sewn-on gear loops. Aside from belaying off it, the belay loop also makes a convenient point to attach a quickdraw and rest on a bolt—when working a route or after a fall. Four gear loops—two on each hip—are enough to hold 20 quickdraws, the maximum number needed for most any clip up.

THE PERFECT FIT

A perfect harness fit might be questionable if you are abnormally gaunt or burly. Try on several to get the right fit—snug but unrestricted. For both women and men who cannot attain the desired fit: Several manufacturers make  "harnesses" where the waist belts and leg loops are fitted and sold separately. By buying a component-based system, you usually can find a satisfactory fit. A kind fit means comfort; it also means that no matter what your body position, the harness will not clench at your rump, constrict leg movement or pinch at the waist. Virtually all quality American- and European-made harnesses have these qualities, but just the same, if you're considering a model or brand unfamiliar to you, try it on, do a couple of deep knee bends and so forth, and see how it feels. A harness is a very personal, specialized piece of gear, so the general craftsmanship should reflect this.

If you're into working routes—hanging on the rope to boulder out the moves—consider something other than the lightest models, which have the least padding. For hangdogging and working routes, buy a sturdy, heavily padded harness—one made for multi-pitch routes. The difference in weight is negligible, but the difference in comfort—when you're hanging in it—can be significant.

Even up to a of couple years ago, you could buy a harness that featured a tie-in point so low that when hanging in the harness, it was difficult to stay upright. These designs have disappeared for the most part, but not entirely. Because

Low-cut sport shoes with good sensitivity and a tapered toe come into their own for working pockets.

Sensitive and flexible, slippers turn your feet into monkey paws, letting you grab, push and pull against the rock featues.

falling is such an integral part of clip-and-go climbing, whatever harness you buy should suspended you upright after a fall. This is normally accomplished by making sure the tie-in point is near, or at, the waist.

A real consideration is price. A $300 ermine-lined poofter harness from France will not get you up any more routes than a $60, made-in-America model with the same practical features.

HAGGARD HARNESS

Because harnesses are made of nylon and are stitched together, they do wear out. Though instances of harnesses breaking are almost unheard of, there's no need to pad the list. Once your harness starts looking even remotely tattered, retire it. The bar-tacked stitching is stronger than the material—at first. Ultraviolet radiation and scuffing are the main culprits of material breakdown. Watch the "hot-spot"—the tie-in area, where the constant tying and untying of the rope, and pulling the rope through, can saw through the material in as little as one season.

ROCK SHOES AND SHOE CARE

A well-fitted high-performance shoe, appropriate for the terrain you're on, is a prerequisite for all serious sport climbers. Dozens of brands and models are currently available. Virtually every contemporary high-performance shoe is cut low around the ankle. High-top boots are for beginners, crack climbing and big walls.

If you travel to various crags, have two, three, or even more styles of shoes to chose from. Go with slippers for bouldering, steep sport climbing and gym climbing, because they're sensitive and allow you to grab with your toes. Also, because at many sport-climbing areas you can bag one route, move ten feet left and bag another, it is superb to be able to pull those shoes off—a snap with the slippers—while resting or waiting for your next try. Pointy slippers, or shoes for pocket routes, are also a necessity. For steep, thin cranking, go with a shoe that has good lateral stiffness. Several models feature plastic inserts specifically for thin edging, but watch out: inserts generally make the shoes too stiff and insensitive for smearing. Shoes without midsoles, or with very thin midsoles, are best for feeling tiny bumps and edges, as well as for extremely overhanging routes where feet act primarily as tentacles, pulling in on the holds. Shoes with beefy midsoles are better suited for edging routes, where the feet bear more of the load.

High performance rock shoes, from the top: a slingshot toe-down shoe, a low-top edging shoe, and a slingshot slipper.

HARDER THE ROUTE, TIGHTER THE SHOES

Most shoes have liners to inhibit stretching; but they stretch a little nonetheless, particularly around the pressure points. Make sure to fit them tight, though not so tight that your toes are bitterly curled in the toe box—unless you're climbing at a very high standard. Shoes eventually mold to your foot, so after a few hours or days, a new pair should become somewhat comfortable, or at least tolerable. Shoes with rubber "slingshot" or "tensioned" rands that extend around the heel, or those with excessive camber, may never be cozy because the rand and/or last design will always drive your toes into

Equipment: Rock Shoes and Shoe Care • 9

the end of the boots. With your toes scrunched, you can front-point on tiny edges much better than when your toes lie flat in the shoes. But wearing these "end-point" shoes for more than brief periods is torturous.

With all lace-up shoes, make sure the opposing eyelets aren't too close together, so the shoes have room to stretch width-wise. Lace the shoes snugly though not painfully, lest you cut off the blood supply to your feet and get painful foot cramps mid-pitch.

Sport climbers wear their boots with and without socks—sans socks for a better fit and increased sensitivity (though after a time their boots take on a cruel bouquet). Others prefer thin socks, citing better comfort. Try it both ways. Just remember, floppy boots have no place on a difficult sport climb.

GREENBACKS

Considering the $130-plus price tag on many fashionable shoe models, most climbers cycle through their shoes, using older shoes for easier climbs, bouldering and indoor training and new, tighter shoes for hard routes or competitions. Worn shoes can be reincarnated by a rubber re-soler, provided they haven't been ridden too hard. If you plan to re-sole your shoes, make sure not to wear through the rand of the toe-box. Five Ten offers a do-it-yourself re-soling kit, though climbers interested in performance usually opt for a professional resole (most go for around $35).

The sheer number of shoe models now available, combined with manufacturers' marketing hype and boot reviews in magazines, can confound a climber looking to plop down some long green for a new pair of boots. Unfortunately, there is no easy solution to this situation, as even sponsored climbers are constantly trying different shoes in the quest for the perfect fit. They'll never find it. Tight shoes will never feel like moccasins.

SAVE YOUR SOLE

Clean all soles before lacing up. Sticky rubber grabs dust, gravel and dirt, but it won't grab the rock very well unless you scrub the trash off it. A quick wash job with spit or plain water, followed by rubbing the soles together till they heat up a tad, will greatly increase a boot's friction. Also, keep your soles free of chalk, which acts as a kind of lubricant, causing the dreaded ball-bearing effect. Do not hike around in your shoes unless absolutely necessary. After a day of climbing, when the boots are moist from sweat, unlace them and air them out in a cool place, otherwise the leather gets brittle and the stitching rots. Never store your boots in the sun—rather in a cool, shady place. Some climbers use a little foot powder; most can't be bothered.

BELAY DEVICES

Belaying someone on a sport climb usually means spending a lot of time holding that person on tension. Performing the task safely and without zapping your hand strength—which you'll need for your own burn—requires a belay device that clamps down, yet also allows you to feed rope or reel in slack in an instant.

Belay devices abound, but only a handful are fit for sport climbing. The proven devices are the Sticht, figure eight and tube types, which cost around $20, and the Petzl Gri-Gri, which costs $70.

Sticht plates (Sticht is a brand name, but we use it generically since numerous companies make belay devices of the same or similar design) lock down the best, and come with or without a spring. Both types work well once you get used to

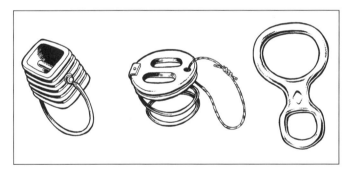

Common belay devices (from left): Tuber type, Sticht plate (with spring), and a figure eight rappel device.

them, but the spring model is more user-friendly, as it doesn't accidentally lockup when the rope is speeding through it.

Figure eights work more smoothly than Sticht plates, provided you belay with a bight of rope passed through the small hole (Sticht-style). Belaying with the rope wound around the figure eight (rappel-style) kinks the rope and yields so much drag that pulling slack out or hauling it in is like hand-hauling a tugboat anchor. Running the rope through the big hole is a treacherous solution. This practice, while speedy, generates far too little holding power.

Before buying a figure eight for belaying, check the instructions and make sure it is designed for the task. Some figure eights are made only for rappelling, having a small hole that's either too small or large to handle belaying.

Lowe Alpine Systems, Black Diamond and Trango all make similar "tube"-type belay/rappel devices. These work much the same as a springless Sticht plate, but have more metal to help dissipate the heat generated when rappelling— a feature seldom needed in sport climbing.

LE GRI GRI

The Petzl Gri-Gri is fast becoming the belay device of choice. This handy unit works similar to a jumar, in that a rotating cam locks down on the rope. The Gri-Gri works automatically: a sharp tug on the rope engages the cam, preventing rope from slipping through. The main benefits of the Gri-Gri are that you can hold someone on tension with virtually no effort, and should you doze off when the leader rips, the device will catch him just the same.

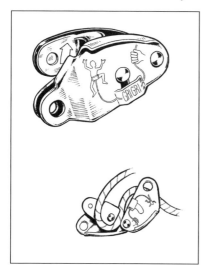

Effective Gri-Gri use takes practice, so don't be surprised if at first the device grabs on you. It also requires a supple rope in the 10-mm range. Stiff, dry ropes won't feed properly, if they feed at all. Cords that are too thick or too slender will either jam up, or won't lock.

The Gri-Gri is fairly foolproof, but load the rope in backward or brake with the wrong hand and your partner can hit the deck. Watch out and pay attention. Read all instructions carefully. Better yet, have someone familiar with the device explain and demonstrate its proper use. If possible, wire its usage in the gym—it only takes perhaps one outing to get it down.

Petzl Gri-Gri

CHAPTER 6

BOLTS

Modern sport-climbing routes do not feature the old-style Rawl Drive bolts, or any quarter-inch diameter bolt (presently referred to as "coffin nails"). The modern standard calls for expansion bolts ⅜ - to ½-inch in diameter. The Rawl 5-piece is the most popular bolt on the American scene today.

The Rawl 5-piece is a "pull-out"-type bolt that pulls a cone into an expanding sleeve as you crank on the bolt head with a wrench, and is one of the best rock bolts available. It has ample strength (7,900 pounds sheer strength for the ⅜-inch), is suitable for a variety of rock surfaces and is relatively foolproof to install. Modest cost, availability, straightforward installation and general reliability has made the Rawl 5-piece the bolt of choice.

The Rawl 5-piece

HANGERS

With the meteoric rise in the popularity of sport climbing has come a slew of new bolt hanger designs, ranging from primitive homemade jobs to slick, brawny commercial hangers. Any of the trade hangers are certain to meet required specifications; homemade hangers may or may not. Aluminum hangers, homemade or otherwise, should be considered suspect if they have taken repeated high-force falls, as the soft material bends and fatigues easily. Always eyeball suspect hangers for cracks or other deformation. Titanium or stainless steel are the best materials for hangers, and comprise almost all of today's fare. Metolius has led the current trend to minimize visual impact by offering three versions of camouflaged stainless steel hangers. If not using these, responsible first ascensionists are painting hangers to match the color of the rock. Trango USA recently has begun importing a highly corrosion-resistant, strong and super light Russian titanium hanger. Petzl, Blue Water and SMC (along with a handful of other companies) also make respectable hangers.

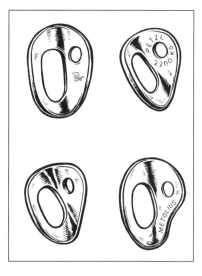

Bolt hangers (clockwise from top left): Blue Water, Petzl, Metolius, and Trango.

Hangers from Hell

Homemade hangers run the gamut from sawed-off and drilled angle iron to double links of chain. As mentioned, some are good, some are not—it's the Devil's guess. Many of the older homemades—nicknamed "pop-offs"—feature a design, like the claw on a hammer, that converts the down-

Lidija Painkiher on Holey Power, 5.13a, Limestone Crag, Kern River, California.

Kevin Powell photo

ward pull of a falling climber into an outward pull on the bolt stud, which could prove disastrous with an old quarter-inch contraction bolt. Beware of any hanger that levers the bolt outward.

SHUT IT

A recent trend at some sport-climbing areas has been to use construction cold shuts (hooks) for hangers—either open for lowering stations, or closed or welded for protection. The advantage of cold shuts is their relatively large diameter and rounded surface, which allows the rope to be placed directly through the hanger for lowering (and does not chew up biners). Two, open cold shuts are fixed at the tops of many routes. When finishing the climb, climbers can simply drape the rope through the open shuts and lower off. Though the folks who install them swear by them, others are leery—and rightly so—to toprope off them. Closed cold shuts may be adequate for lowering and toproping, but they are debatable for lead protection.

BOLT TEST

While clinging to a ghastly sport route by one hand, there is no absolutely reliable method to test in situ bolts, but there are plenty of reasons to want to. Here are some considerations and suggestions:

- Unlike the quarter-inch "coffin nails" of traditional, bolted-on-the-lead routes, nearly all bolts on modern clip-and-go routes are industrial-strength ⅜- or ½-inch units strong enough to tether off a battleship. Still, don't blindly trust any bolt, especially one that, if it failed, would result in your "grounding out" (hitting the deck) or smacking a ledge.

- Give each bolt a quick eyeballing. Consider any bolt less than ⅜-inch in diameter suspect. Make sure the bolt is snug in the hole and the hanger is snug against the rock. A bolt that is sticking part of the way out and a hanger that spins are signs that the bolt was improperly installed, or has crept loose. While poorly placed ⅜- and ½-inch bolts probably will hold a savage fall, don't count it. Rather, back off. If a hanger is merely loose, haul up a wrench and snug down the bolt. Expansion bolts, like the Rawl and Hilti, loosen over time or after repeated falls. It usually takes years for a sound bolt to work loose, but in soft rock, like the welded tuff of Smith Rock, bolts can loosen in as little as one season. Bolts that tighten up are no problem; but if the bolt turns without drawing tight, the threads are likely stripped and the bolt needs replacing—a job for experienced climbers only.

- Never hammer on a bolt—doing so will only damage the head and hanger.

- If the rock around the bolt head has flaked away ("cratering"), or the bolt shank is bent, assume that the bolt can no longer hold a fall and take the necessary precautions by either backing up the bolt or retreating.

- Some rust on the bolt head and hanger is common and doesn't necessarily signal a weakened placement. However, deeply pitted bolts and hangers—which are common on sea cliffs—are highly suspect, and need replacing with more corrosion-resistant stainless steel bolts.

- Remember, a bolt is only as strong as the rock that it's set in, so examine the rock around the bolt. If it sounds hollow, or is overly fractured, beware. Also, watch out for bolts set in big "boiler plates" or blocks, either of which can come off in your lap.

BINERS AND QUICKDRAWS

CHAPTER 7

CARABINERS

Your main carabiner is a big locking one for belaying. A large-diameter, pear-shaped unit is best. This biner will last years, and is roomy enough to clip to the belay loop on your harness and still hold a bight of rope. The locking portion of the biner can be either a screw gate, or an auto-lock. I prefer auto-lock biners because they are always locked, and are a tad easier to deal with once you get a feel for feathering the sleeve/lock widget. Screw gates work just as well, but the locking collars can seize up, requiring pliers to release them. Keep all carabiners clean (dirt will impede the lock), and discard them once they show signs of grooving.

auto-lock gate biner

DRAWS

Sport climbing does not require much hardware, but a good selection of quickdraws are essential. Fifteen to 20 is the magic number. You can go on the cheap and tie your own draws, but knotted jobs don't work as well as commercially sewn ones, and are weaker besides.

The standard quickdraw length is four inches. These "shorties" should constitute 80 percent of your selection, and are used mostly for clipping bolts. To reduce rope drag, have a few longer ones on hand for clipping pro under roofs or at the start of traverses. Quality draws come with a rubber sleeve or band that pins the bottom carabiner in place, preventing it from flipping around when clipping in. For tied draws, a couple of wraps of cloth tape will work in place of the rubber sleeve.

screw gate biner

Rigging Draws

Rig your draws with a modified-D carabiner on the top to clip bolts, and a bent-gate D on the bottom to clip the rope. Modified-Ds are strong and light; the crook in the bent-gate units makes dropping in the rope a snap. Do not clip a bolt with a bent-gate carabiner, as the bend can cause the biner to unclip itself. Disregard "superlight" biners. They cut a couple ounces off your rack, but their thin stock chews up ropes, and can even skin the sheath right off if the line tracks across the spine of the biner. Better to go with slightly heavier biners, made from large-diameter aluminum stock that's easy on the rope. Bolt hangers

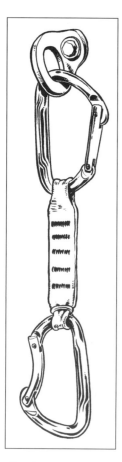

Place bent-gate cara-biners on the bottom of the quickdraw and pin it in place with a rubber band. A quickdraw rigged in this manner is easy to clip, and the bottom carabiner won't flip around.

are notoriously hard on biners, so periodically examine them and discard ones that are deeply gouged.

PARA-
PHERNALIA

CHAPTER 8

CLOTHES

Climbing in Levis is out. Regular exercise cloths are suitable. Most climbers prefer the freedom of shorts or 3/4-length tights, temperature permitting. Fit should not be restrictive, but should be close. Avoid clothes that are so loose they can become entangled in the gear, or balloon out so far you can't see your feet. Tight-fitting stretchy fabrics, like cotton/spandex blends, are most functional and comely—if it's warm enough.

Several manufacturers have designed clothing specifically for sport climbing. The accent is on style and function, and if you've the greenbacks, this may be the best way to go. However, I have never heard of a climber failing on a bleak route because he or she was wearing the wrong threads. A reasonably tight-fitting shirt and a simple pair of stretch pants/shorts is the standard getup. Layer your clothes in colder weather.

CHALK BAG AND CHALK

Some climbers favor block chalk over powdered chalk. It's all basically the same stuff (carbonate of magnesium), though some brands stick better to sweaty mits. The "best" type is your preference. If one kind feels slippery, dump it out and try another brand. The stuff is cheap enough. The chalk ball—a small porous bag containing chalk—is required in many climbing gyms owing to near white-out conditions that can result from all the chalk dust. Outdoors, many climbers find the chalk ball less effective, preferring to simply dip their hands in a chalk bag and instantly be chalked up. The chalk ball must be kneaded. Various forms of "ecochalk," in natural rock colors, have as yet not managed to solve the problem of the pigments, which tend to make the chalk slippery, and can stain your duds as well as the rock.

It seems everyone with a sewing machine makes chalk bags. Any decent bag should feature a drawstring on the top to cinch the bag tightly shut. Even then, chalk will get on everything. (Many climbers clip their chalk bags on the *outside* of their packs.) The mouth of the bag must be a little bigger than your hand—to allow quick and easy entry—and should be of the "stay open" variety. This is normally accomplished with a wire sewn or fitted around the top of the opening. The bag should also feature a wide and sturdy loop, attached high on the bag, through which to feed a waist sling.

Beyond this, the rest is a matter of preference and style. Most climbers secure bags to their waists via thin webbing or cordage, secured with a square knot or a small plastic fastbuckle. Cinch the loop snug, but not tight. I (J.L.) like to move the knot to the middle of my back so I can freely slide the bag around on the sling. You don't want to reach across your body to chalk up. Though I've never liked this method, many climbers keep their bags behind them, out of the way. They need only reach back and dip. Whatever method you come to use, always do it the same way, so the procedure is automatic, and you're not left crimping that dime fumbling for a dip.

BRUSHES

Most chalk bags have a little sleeve sewn onto the side to accommodate a stiff bristled nylon brush, used primarily to brush off chalk-caked holds. A toothbrush is the standard unit, though a slightly larger article, like a nylon grout brush, is better. Wire brushes, the kind used to remove rust from steel, are also popular for knocking off lichen and loose grit. The drawback is that these brushes can actually scar soft rock, and on granite and limestone, they tend to leave a gray, metallic sheen on the holds, making them more slippery than before.

TAPE

A roll of one-inch athletic (cloth) tape is standard gear for all sport climbers. Curity makes the stickiest brand. Stay away from "plastic" or "waterproof" tape; it is sweaty and doesn't stick.

The most common use for tape is to support sore fingers/tendons with a couple of thin wraps on either side of the second knuckle. Tape also comes in handy for covering abrasions and split fingertips, and for any number of other uses. Simply tear the tape to the size desired.

TAPING BASES

For use on skin: Tape works most effectively if you first treat the skin with a dab of tincture of benzoin, which helps the tape adhere and keep it from rolling at the edges when your fingers contact the rock. Other fancy taping bases are available. Some, like the popular Tuff-Skin and Mueller Clear Spray, come in aerosol cans; but a little bottle of benzoin is cheap and works just as well as the more pricey potions. The one danger of all taping bases is the container they come in. Glass breaks. The plastic bottles usually have cheap, two-thread caps that leak. The lid often comes off the aerosol cans, and a little pressure on the nozzle can activate the

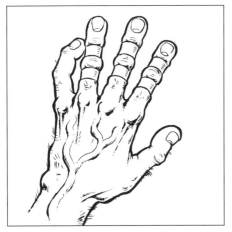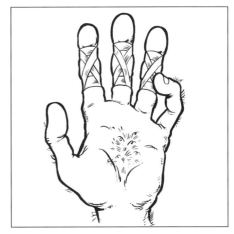

works. Whatever, if a taping base leaks or sprays out in your pack, it's like hosing bong water over your white linen pants. You'll need a blowtorch to get it off your hardware, and all software—cloths, slings and pack—are permanently stained. If you're going to use a taping base, buy a little poly bottle with a bombproof top to store it in, or tape the top shut on the cans.

CRASH PADS

Hard core boulderers have long used a small carpet, or "sketch pad," as a starting platform on the ground at the base of the problem. Many pads feature thick foam for cushioning long bouldering falls. Sketch pads work equally well as launching pads for grim sport climbs, where a clean sole is advised, and where you might want some cushioning for crux opening moves—just in case you ping off.

Black Diamond and Kinnaloa make sketch pads that sell for between $100 and $200. It follows that most climbers fashion their own. A standard pad features a two-foot square piece of two-inch-thick foam, sandwiched between tough-gauge nylon that can withstand grating over rough rock and a stomping. The nylon is stitched around the foam like a pillowcase, though most climbers glue the foam to the skin as well—to keep the foam from bunching up. The better units are actually two of these covered pads connected with a nylon hinge, so the rig can be folded up and carried around like a briefcase (affix a nylon handle). These pads might not help much on a bad fall, but they are a godsend when jumping off onto uneven ground, and all but eliminate nasty heel bruises and ankle tweaks from low-level falls.

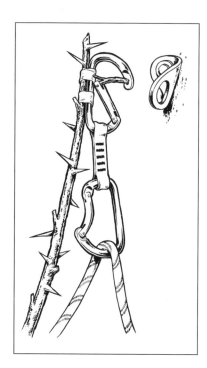

STICK-CLIP STICK

On numerous sport routes, the first bolt is intentionally set higher than you can clip from the ground. You can risk your neck getting to that bolt, but savvy climbers snare it via a stick clip. The stick clip rig is basic: All you need is a stout stick (or tent pole) of the appropriate length, a quickdraw, and cloth tape.

Work a stick clip this way: Tape the top carabiner on the quickdraw snugly to the end of the stick. Next, wedge a twig into its gate to hold it open. Clip the rope into the bottom bent-gate. Hoist the rig to the out-of-reach bolt, and snare it. The top carabiner gate should snap shut. A jerk on the stick releases it from the quickdraw. Now, with the rope clipped securely overhead, you can fearlessly grapple with the opening moves.

Epic, out of Salt Lake City, makes a product called the "Stick Clip"—a pair of nylon jaws that replace the tape and the twig and work better as well. The unit sells for about $6—just add the stick.

PROCEDURES

CHAPTER 9

BELAYING

Belaying on sport routes is demanding work, requiring precise communication and teamwork between leader and belayer.

I (D.R.) learned this the hard way while trying to lead Might As Well Pump, a severely overhanging face route at Independence Pass, just outside Aspen, Colorado. The climbing was mid-5.12, my max for on-sight leading.

Everything went splendidly up to the fifth bolt. Just above loomed the crux, a series of greasy granite slopers. Clipping that fifth bolt required a hateful one-arm hang from a burnished carbuncle which, even had I been fresh, would have pressed me. Instantly pumped, only steel will would get the quickdraw on and the rope clipped before I blew.

I psyched, crimped the carbuncle earnestly, snagged a draw off my harness and snapped it onto the bolt. Cramps

Sport climbing isn't for slackers, and demands constant concentration from both leader and belayer. A good, astute belayer stands tall and watches the leader to anticipate his movements, as shown by Paul Clark as he belays Jack Mileski on a steep pocket route outside Waco, Texas.

Keeping attentive is an essential skill as a belayer.

racked my legs; my hand palsied on the carbuncle. No way was I going to get the rope in clean. Forgetting about flashing the route, I grabbed the bottom biner on the draw and, with my free hand, pulled for slack. Nothing doing. The cord was drawn tight as a bowstring. I yanked again. This time the slack came. I cursed savagely and clipped the rope in. Lisa, my belayer and wife, heard my yell and, thinking I was off, pulled the rope taut, crushing my fingers in the bottom of the biner. I cursed again, tearing my hand loose. Unfortunately, the rope popped free with my mangled fingers.

Hearing my second cry, Lisa thought I wanted slack and fed out a generous dosage. And I was off, hurtling past the lower bolts to finally wrench to a stop barely three feet off the deck. Had the route not been so steep I could have lost considerable hide—at the very least—all for not communicating with my belayer.

Good communication between leader and belayer is the first rule of business. On sport routes the commands are few and simple. When the leader cries, "Slack," feed out enough rope for him to either make the clip, or execute the next move without rope drag. "Up rope"—reel some back in. "Take" means the leader wants you to hold him on tension. In that case, pull the rope tight, lock your belay device and pull some more. When the leader wishes to resume climbing, he'll either say, "Slack," or "Climbing." The final signal is "Falling." When you hear that, lock the belay device and brace for impact.

Besides listening for the commands, watch the leader to *anticipate* when he needs slack; prepare to catch him when he looks shaky. These duties are requisite of a good sport belayer, and are impossible when you're sitting or lying down, or are in la-la land. A good belayer is vigilant, on his toes and always faces the leader.

Belay position is likewise crucial. It usually is best to stand directly beneath the first protection bolt. Shiftless, irresponsible and harebrained belayers hang out well off to the side, or far back from the wall—and get keelhauled through the talus when the leader pings, dropping him needlessly far—or worse, they lose control and drop the leader clear to the deck. Disaster. Because of the close proximity of bolts on most clip-and-go routes, climbers sometimes forego a belay anchor when the belay is on the ground. However, when the disparity of weight between leader and belayer is considerable, or when the leader is "working" a route, or when the base is uneven or loose, anchor up (directly beneath the first protection bolt) if at all possible.

TOUCH

Developing a knack for how much slack you need in the rope requires practice and a certain touch. As a rule, if you can feel the climber move through the rope, or if the cord tugs against your belay device, it's too tight. A properly fed rope hangs limp in the quickdraws, like laundry on the line. At bolt clips, the leader needs about four feet of slack, usually pulled up in two bights—so be ready. Lunges and dynamic moves also require instant slack, so again, stay sharp. When in doubt, belay as you'd like to be belayed.

After you fall on the steep, getting re-established involves self-pulleying yourself up while the belayer locks the belay device and leans or walks back to help winch you up.

TWO STEP

You can feed rope in or out by working it though the belay device, but it's usually faster and easier to stand a couple of paces away from the base of the climb and step forward to give slack, or step back to take in rope. This technique requires going without a belay anchor, a practice that goes against the traditional climbing grain. Not anchoring in, while a death-defying practice on multi-pitch routes, is, as mentioned, a common practice on sport routes—*provided the leader and belayer are approximately the same weight, and the belayer is positioned close to the wall and directly beneath the first pro.* Just the same, belaying without an anchor is always a calculated risk—it's your call.

When belaying someone who outweighs you, set a stout, multi-directional belay anchor or, in the event of a fall, risk getting extruded through the first quickdraw and dropping the leader that much further.

"FALLING!"

When the leader falls, the belayer has three options. You can simply stand there and catch him, which is the norm. Even better, as you feel the rope being loaded, jump up to lessen the impact on the leader and the bolts. When the leader is in danger of, say, smacking into the lip of a roof, reel out enough slack to enable him to fall clear of the obstacle. The leader may blaspheme you for dropping him the extra distance, but that's much preferred to fetching the meat wagon.

ON THE STEEP

When the leader pops on an overhanging route, the belayer usually has to help winch him back up to the high point. To do this, simply lock your belay device and walk away from the wall, as the leader hauls down on the rope running back to the belay. Again, this procedure requires no belay anchor. If the route is so steep that the leader hangs in space, the belayer has to help "snap" him up the rope. Again, lock the belay device and lean back so you are pulling on the rope. The leader should grab the rope overhead, execute a quick chin-up, then release the rope. Your counterweight will snap the slack out and the leader will gain a couple of feet. Repeat the process until the leader is back on the rock.

More of these techniques will be covered in the section on "Working a Route." For now, understand that while clip-and-go climbing is often interpreted as a "safe" venture—which is not necessarily true—belaying remains just as crucial as on the wildest adventure climbs. Just because there often are bolts every six or so feet doesn't preclude a leader from grounding out if the belay fails. A *cavalier* attitude toward belaying is a certain recipe for disaster, especially on clip-and-go routes, where falling is so routine. Everyone communicates a little differently, so when tackling a route near your limit, try to get a belayer you are familiar with, and who is familiar with you.

SELECTING A ROUTE

Up until about 1980, there was never much of a problem with climbers trying routes supposedly, or actually, too hard for them. The lack of pro, the exposure and the frank commitment let climbers know quickly and viscerally when they were entering no-man's land, and they would simply retreat. Much was written about not getting in over your head and getting hurt, but in fact the manifest terror of doing so was the greatest safeguard against it happening in all but isolated cases. With clip-and-go routes, however, where the routes are mostly short and the bolts plentiful, there's no risk at all, right? Wrong.

The problem is not that most clip-and-go routes are inherently dangerous. Most of them are not—provided you know precisely what you are doing, and stick religiously to the safety fundamentals. The snag is that climbers who were essentially reared in the gym and who haven't acquired the wherewithal from working through the grades on traditional routes, are making untoward mistakes, most of them avoidable. More on this shortly, in the section on **Climbing, Clipping and Lowering.**

MAXED

The entire psychology of sport climbing is the pursuit of difficulty, so trying routes that are two, even three letter grades above your perceived limit is routine. There are both advantages and disadvantages to doing so.

You will never find your limit until you try to exceed it. Attempting a route harder than you have so far accomplished can be instructional. It gives a tangible gauge of where you're at technically, can help overcome the imposing aura of high numbers, can be a learning experience about how to "work" a route and, if nothing else, is usually a good workout. Top climbers invariably focus on climbs supposedly too hard for them, written off as impossible by everyone else, or never even considered. Such is how standards rise. But for both intermediate and world-class sport climbers, spending too much time working routes can adversely effect your climbing style and ultimately, can even lower performance—to say nothing of reducing the experience to bitter toil on 10 feet of rock. There is also the physiological fact that no one can perform at maximum level every day. World-class sprinters, for instance, only run all out during races. Most all their training

(opposite page)
Tim Wagner on Mentor, 5.12a, Virgin River Gorge, Arizona.
Tim Powell photo

Route Selection:

- No one can climb at his or her limit every day, so don't try to.

- The techniques and demands of different routes vary dramatically. Just because you have accomplished a 5.12b thin hold route does not mean you won't get spanked on a 5.11d climb up an overhanging line of slopers.

- While it is gratifying to stick with your forté (pocket climbs, crimper routes, and so forth), strive to become an overall climber by *working on your weaknesses*. Drop down a couple of letter grades and get the feeling and satisfaction of dusting off a route featuring a technique you are deficient at.

- Vary the difficulty and the medium (granite, limestone, welded tuff, and so forth) to keep the experience novel and exciting.

- Pick a "project" route that is too hard, and work on it over a period of time.

- Spend part of each outing flashing easier routes. A flash ascent is the preferred conclusion to any climb, so stay sharp on this skill by practicing it often.

- Always put the highest premium on fun and companionship. There is no real money in climbing, but the very experience, shared with friends, is priceless.

is done at 80 to 90 percent of maximum.

Sure, if the risks seem manageable—and this is purely your call—challenge yourself on difficult routes. Just make certain to phase maximum efforts with plenty of doable, even moderate, climbing.

RIVER RUNS THROUGH IT

Bouldering problems usually can be reduced to individual moves or small sequences. Not so with proper routes. Even on routes as short as 40 or 50 feet, rhythm and flow enter the equation in a big way. Spend too much time frigging and dogging your way up routes and you will lose the liquid flow and all sense of spontaneity, because your instincts are numbed by too much thinking and fiddling. It is also frustrating. Refinements in technique usually come from mastering manageable problems. The professional baseball player does not take batting practice from someone throwing the ball 90 miles per hour—more like 60 miles per hour, and right over the plate. This way, the batter can get serious wood on the ball and "find his swing" if he's slumping, or really hone in if he's not. Inch up the difficulty as mastery increases; drop down a grade if your form is off. Look at boxing. They don't throw a 20-year old hopeful in the ring with the world champion. He'd likely get his ass kicked so thoroughly that he'd never get over it. Sure, get in over your head if the pro is bomber and you feel sharp. But be realistic. Trying to jump up more than a couple letter grades—say, from 5.10c to 5.11b—is bound to be more discouraging than instructional.

CHAPTER 11

CLIMBING, CLIPPING AND lOWERING

Sport climbing is inherently simple; the gear is minimal and the techniques spare. It is not, however, a brainless activity.

Several years ago I (D.R.) was climbing at American Fork, a trendy sport crag outside Salt Lake City. My partner was Conrad Anker, an accomplished big-wall and alpine climber. I'd just led an overhanging pitch and Conrad was following, cleaning the quickdraws as he went. Twenty-five feet up,

Lisa Raleigh positions the rope in the quickdraw so that the gate faces away from the direction of travel.

"J.L.'s RISK-O-METER"

For any given stretch of climbing, ask yourself these questions:

• What is the protection, and is there any chance of it failing if I fall before getting to the next pro. With clip-and-go routes, the pro is primarily bolts, closely (but not always) spaced. It is uncommon—though *not* unheard of—that one of these bolts will fail, so this is rarely a factor.

• What is the longest possible fall I can take before I gain the next bolt? Double the runout and add five feet. If the runout is eight feet, you might fall 20 feet and change.

• Determine what, if anything, you might hit if you fall. A 20-foot fall is no joke, and something as small as a rounded horn or a two-inch shelf can snag a foot and snap it. If the wall below is steep and smooth, the fall will probably be uneventful—provided the climbing does not traverse, and the wall is not too overhanging.

Know the consequences and be prepared for these conditions:

• Climbing that goes even slightly sideways can have a pendulum effect in a fall. In addition, momentum will want to spin you while you are swinging back into plumb. Keep your wits and don't freeze up. Assume a cat-like position, feet and hands spread apart, keeping your head and torso away from the rock.

• If the wall is severely overhanging and you ping off, you run the risk of swinging back into the wall and smacking it. Assume the cat-like position, and absorb any impact with bent arms and legs.

If all points check out on the risk-o-meter, and you follow basic safety procedures, the risks are probably manageable (though nothing is assured in climbing), whether the route is 5.10a or 5.14. In most, but not all cases, the harder the route, the better the pro.

Conrad hit the crux, a run of blocky grey jugs that stepped out like an inverted staircase. As he began the moves I hauled on the rope to snug it up, and in doing so pulled the rope loose from Conrad's harness: his knot had come untied. In Conrad's haste to follow the pitch—a climb that was easy for him and one he'd done many times before—he had neglected to follow his tie-in knot back through, distracted perhaps by our conversation about *Zorro* reruns and home brewing.

I warned Conrad who, now scared shitless, was just able to snag a quickdraw off his harness and anchor into a bolt. He tied back in, and after a moments rest to retrieve his mind, followed the pitch.

Other climbers, like Lynn Hill, haven't been so lucky. Lowering off a sport climb in France, she learned how important it is to pay attention to details when her knot became untied. She fell 60 feet and hit the ground (remarkably escaping with only abrasions and a dislocated elbow). The lesson is: Before you climb or lower, check your knot. When you tie in, concentrate on what you're doing. Don't wax about *Zorro* or fiddle with anything else until that knot is finished. It doesn't matter if you're preparing to lower, toprope, or lead. Always stay sharp—or give up your ghost.

Before casting off on the lead, run through the following checklist:

• Are my shoes snugged up and clean? A quick spit-cleaning will make the rubber especially sticky.

• Is my harness and tie-in knot secure?

• Do I have enough quickdraws (carry at least two more than you think you'll need), and are they racked where I can fetch them quickly?

• Is the first bolt stick, or double clipped if needed?

• Is the belayer ready? Is the rope laid out cleanly?

• Is my chalk bag full and open?

Provided you know and follow basic safety fundamentals, there is a simple formula (left) you can apply to most any clip-and-go lead and know—not perfectly, but reasonably well—what the risks are.

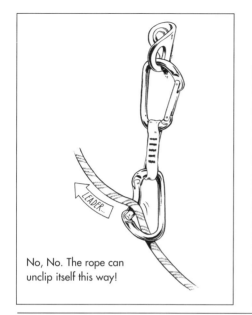

No, No. The rope can
unclip itself this way!

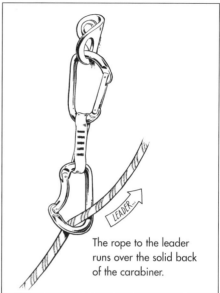

The rope to the leader
runs over the solid back
of the carabiner.

CLIPPING

Sport climbs, or clip-and-go routes, are always bolt-protected;
and there are right and wrong ways to clip bolts.

Common sense tells you to clip a bolt as soon as it's within reach. This is normally correct. Sometimes, however, the
holds directly below a bolt are too lean to hang from by one
hand while hauling up slack for the clip. In this case, consider climbing higher to better holds—if available—then reaching down to make the clip. Sure, you'll fall several feet further
if you blow off, but if you're hanging from that sinker jug, the
odds of pinging are far more remote than if you've paused to
crimp some dreary nubbin.

Key when clipping a bolt: Set the quickdraw so the gate on
the bottom carabiner (the rope end) faces away from your
line of travel. For instance, if you plan to traverse left above a
bolt, clip the draw so the bottom carabiner faces to the right,
and vice versa if you're cranking the other way. Facing the
gate away from your line of travel will help keep the rope from
backtracking over the gate and coming unclipped—a real pos-
sibility with the bent-gate biners normally used to clip the
rope on sport climbs.

There are two ways to clip a biner into a bolt: the finger clip
and the thumb clip. The thumb clip is preferred. Four fingers
stabilize the biner on the off-gate side, and it's a natural move
to depress the gate with the thumb. Rack your draws for
thumb-clipping.

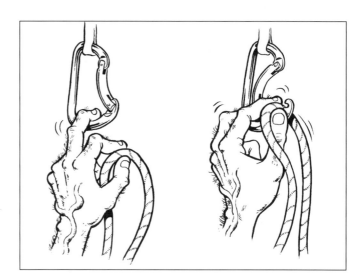

Finger clip

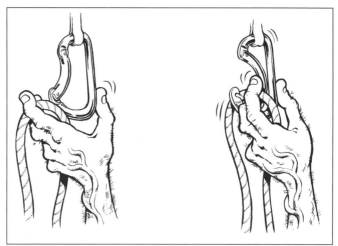

Thumb clip

High Bolt

Certain climbs, usually ones with crux opening moves, have the first bolt intentionally set well off the deck. Here, break out your "cheater" stick and clip that sucker from the ground. When there's a chance the bolt—or any other bolt for that matter—might come unclipped, use locking biners, or clip the bolt and rope with two quickdraws (double clip).

LOWERING

Most sport-climbing accidents occur *after* the climb, and are related to lowering or rappelling. Tying back in improperly after threading the rope through the lowering anchors accounts for the majority of accidents, some of them fatal and none of them minor. A moment's inattentiveness caused by the elation of success, or any brief distraction, is all that is

neeeded for you to forget to finish your tie-in knot, or unclip from the anchors and lean back without warning your belayer. Never simply drop back onto the rope, assuming the belayer has you "on." I (J.L.) like to not only vocally verify the

Christina Jackson going for the clip on Pigs in Zen, 5.12a, Crystal River valley, Colorado.

1.

2.

Lowering from the fixed anchor:

1. Clip into the anchor chains above their end with quickdraws. Get some slack, tie a figure eight in the rope.

2. Clip the figure eight into your harness, untie from the end of the rope and pass that end through the ends of the chain anchors.

belay, but to also *feel* the tension at my waist before I even unclip to lower off. Doublecheck everything. It only takes seconds.

Develop a working system and stick to it. Just as you tie in and rack the same way, get a routine down for lowering. Every time you top out, clip to the lowering station, untie, thread and tie back in—always perform each of these procedures the exact same way. Doing so greatly reduces your chances of making a fatal mistake.

Smooth Operator

Of the numerous lowering methods, the following is the most foolproof, and works in most situations:

- Examine the lowering station. If any part—the bolts, chain links, rings, hooks, or webbing—looks questionable, replace it or back it up. In the worst case, you can leave the last protection bolt clipped with a single carabiner (as a backup to a suspect lowering station). Nearly all sport climbs are rigged with stations that let you lower when the rope is halfway out; if the station is old, it may only have runners. Here, set up for a rappel, as a rope will burn through nylon slings if you try to lower off them.

- At a proper lowering station, clip to the anchor using two quickdraws (or runners) that are long enough to let you hang from the bolts without pulling out on them. Clip the quickdraws to either the tie-in section of your harness, or the belay/-rappel loop if your harness has this feature and it's in good condition; then clip the quickdraws to the station. If the station is a snarl of runners and rappel rings, clip through the runners—or the bolt hangers themselves if you can get to them—to free the rings for the rope. If the station is a chain, clip to the links above the bottom ones, which you need free to thread the rope. With open cold-shuts or similar hooks, you need only run the rope across the hook arms and tell your belayer to lower you. Ditto for stations with fixed biners—just clip in and lower.

- After clipping in, call for slack and reel up about five feet of rope. Tie an overhand figure eight knot three to five feet down from your harness knot, then clip this to your harness using the same carabiners you're hanging from or a locking biner carried expressly for the task. Some climbers forgo this step. Don't. You risk dropping the rope once you're untied, or worse, plummeting to the talus if the anchor fails while you're untying or tying back in.

- After you're safely clipped in, untie the rope from your harness, thread the rope through the lowering rings, and tie back in using the same knot you used for leading. That accomplished, unclip from the overhand figure eight, untie it, and tell your belayer to yard out the slack and "take" you. Unclip the quickdraws from the station and lower.

Lowering from the fixed anchor (continued):

3. Tie back into the rope. Untie your temporary figure eight knot, call for your belayer to hold your weight, unclip the quickdraws and get lowered away.

Aerial Tram

On steep routes, "tram" into the rope by clipping a quickdraw to your harness, then to the section of rope running through the bolts. Tramming prevents you from swinging out in space, and makes it easy to retrieve quickdraws and scour the holds on your way down. Watch out as you near the ground, though. Unclipping from the first bolt can send you whistling back into a tree or boulder. If that is possible, stay clipped through the first bolt, lower to the ground, then boulder up to the bolt to retrieve your draw.

Tramming onto the rope
with a biner to keep
from swinging out on the
lower.

FALLING

Clip-and-go climbing is synonymous with falling, so get used to it. Learn to fall the right way, and you'll have a fruitful career.

Sport-climbing falls are usually predictable, hence controllable. Avoid injuries by climbing smartly. Be aware of the rope

Reduce your chances of injury by assuming a relaxed, cat-like position when you fall. Doing so lets you absorb the brunt of the impact with your feet and legs, as shown here by Phil Bram, as he whips off Chinaman's Chance, 5.12c, in the Quartz Mountains of Oklahoma.

to avoid getting tangled in it. When climbing straight up, let the rope hang between your legs. On traverses, you should let the rope run over the top of the trailing thigh to prevent you from catching a leg and spinning in a fall (and remember to assume the cat-like position if you ping off a traverse).

If you know you're going to fall, pick a clean landing zone and aim for it. This may involve climbing a move or two higher, or reversing a move or so, to give you the right trajectory. Falling out of liebacks or heel hooks is dangerous because you tend to fall head first. Be aware of this. Pitching off directly above and close to a bolt might seem casual once you let go, but short falls can slam you into the rock with a vengeance. To soften the impact on short, steep "wrenchers," consider calling for a couple of feet of slack before you pitch off. Absorb the brunt of the impact with your legs.

Reduce the risk of injury by staying upright. Loosely holding onto the knot at your harness can help, but fight the urge to really clamp down on the rope—or get burned. As you fall, relax. A calm, supple body is far less susceptible to injury than a rigid one. And if the thought of falling terrifies you, ease into it. Practice taking short falls (with bomber protection nearby) until you feel comfortable.

As mentioned, you normally know in advance when you're going going to fall. Failing fingers and bungled sequences are the usual predicaments. But sometimes a toe will blow off a hold, a hand will slip, or you'll botch a dead point and wing off unexpectedly. The business about your life flashing before your eyes during a fall is patent hogwash. It all happens much too suddenly. On an out-of-the-blue fall, your best defense against injury is to remain completely relaxed and try to flow into the cat-like stance—legs slightly apart and bent, arms out to get your head and torso away from the rock. Freeze up and expect the worse, because you're probably going to get it.

WORKING A ROUTE

After any fall, take a two- to five-minute rest. If you're totally goosed, lower off; however, it is usually more time and energy efficient to hang from a bolt and rest, then try the move again. The most efficient way to regain the high point is to winch up the rope (a technique discussed under **Belaying**). When the wall is too steep for that, snap back up (also detailed under **Belaying**).

Howie Feinsilber on Apollo Reed, 5.13a, Summersville Lake, New River Gorge, West Virginia.

Kevin Powell photo

Upon regaining your high point, "daisy" into the bolt with a quickdraw clipped to the belay/rappel loop on your harness.

Hanging directly on the rope works as well, but tuckers the belayer's hands. Give him a break. As mentioned, many sport climbers are going with the Gri Gri; this way, when the leader is hanging/resting, the belayer's hands need only lightly squeeze the rope. But if you plan on hanging for more than a quick break, even if the belayer is using a Gri Gri, daisy in to rest.

When resting, analyze why you fell, and devise a solution. Don't have tunnel vision. Elite climbers who work a lot of grim routes commonly try 10 or more ways of doing a move or sequence. The fact that you pumped out of a move doesn't necessarily mean you are too weak to dick it. A faulty sequence may have brought on a premature pump. Always focus on better technique, better feet, better rests, and so on. And move through tough sections decisively and fast. If you pumped out up high, concentrate your efforts on finding a rest, or an easier way to do the lower section. Wiring the lower section of a bleak route is essential, for it allows you to husband your strength for when you most need it—later on.

Ledge and stemming rests are obvious, but never disregard hidden rests, like knee bars, hand stuffs, heel hooks and thumb hooks. These may not always be hands-down, kickback rests, but you'll appreciate every respite once you're back on the sharp end. And remember, the back-step/drop-knee is fundamental to climbing steep rock. Finding one, or several, back-steps during the course of a pitch can make a desperate route feel solid and an impossible route doable.

The vast majority sport climbing falls occur when you're too flamed to hang on; but you can also get a technical spanking. That's right. And a technical spanking manifests in a major pump. So don't be hoodwinked: Your pump may well have resulted from unsuitable technique, not lack of might. To avoid a repeat, inspect the rock for clues—like chalk and rubber skids—that might unlock the sequence. Use your daisy and tension around to feel the holds, then practice the moves on a taut rope. There are usually several ways to crack a crux, but only one is likely the "easy" path. That's the one you want. Hang there and work the moves until you are confident you have found the best progression, the line of least resistance.

FRIGG IT IN REVERSE

Problematic sections may require "frigging" up (a cheater stick helps here) to a higher bolt, clipping in, then working the moves in reverse. You also can do this with tension from a high rope. When you know that you must latch a hold with a certain hand, use that as your starting point and work backward.

Work the route bolt to bolt till you know every move and sequence better than the hair on your palms. Leave nothing

to chance, especially the exit. You will hit the closing moves with a raging death pump, so wire them more so than the rest of the route.

Jeff Jackson copping a foot-stuff rest on steep Texan limestone.

To further increase your chances for a successful redpoint, work the bolt clips just as you do the moves, and mark hidden holds with a dab of chalk (brush it off afterward). If you have trouble remembering moves, draw a route topo to help burn the sequence into your lobes. Better yet, use visualization to help code in the sequence while you're resting. Visualization is fundamental to putting together a hard redpoint. Climbing the route in your mind is almost as beneficial as taking another burn on it bolt to bolt. Finally, try to preserve your mits. Don't hurl yourself at sharp holds till your hands are flayed nubs. Practice sharp or stressful moves as little as possible, or else tape your fingers and, even then, easy does it.

If a climb is right at your limits, you may want to lead it in sections prior to a redpoint try (thus breaking down a long, grisly route into a series of shorter sequences). A good strategy is to dog your way to the last third of the climb, then try to lead it clean from there to the top. Once you dust the upper third, backtrack, and try to lead from a bolt or two lower. Repeat until you're on the ground. Working a route backward—instead of the usual tactic of working from the ground to the top—forces you to climb the exit (where you will be the most spent) more than the start, where, even if it is the crux, you'll at least be fresh.

GASSED

Getting a route thoroughly "sussed" can sap you. If you are gassed, loaf for awhile, do a couple of easier routes to recover, eat an energy bar and drink some water or sports drink to help get some fuel (sugar in the form of glycogen) to your muscles. Or, simply return another day and dust it. Punishing yourself on a route ad nauseam will only break your spirit and promote future failures as, more often than not, you'll only practice the wrong way to do the moves. Likewise, repeating the same heinous move (a monodoigt pocket pull or a lunge to a tweaky edge) more than a couple of times can result in acute injury, which can knock you off the rock for a month or more.

If you have enough juice to pull off a redpoint after working a route, go for it, but first: Untie. Walk around. Rest. Belay your partner on her project. And drink lots of water to keep your muscles and tendons hydrated. Rehearse the moves in your mind, too.

Once you're ready, concentrate on the climb, and only the climb. Don't make stupid mistakes, like clipping the rope in backward. Do the moves as you rehearsed them. A redpoint burn is the wrong time to practice a new sequence, so don't fall into this most common of traps. Stick with what you have found to work. Stay focused and relaxed. Draw a few deep breaths before you cast off, and continue breathing steadily and deeply as you yard through the crux moves. It is very common for a climber to hold his/her breath while cranking hard moves. Remember: No oxygen means no energy production. Keep the carburetor mixture rich. Bear down, remain confident, turn off your thinking mind and climb instinctivly. And quickly. You're better off firing through the route too fast than too slow. Dawdling on steep rock is taxing, so keep it moving. Buen suerte.

TRAINING AND INJURIES

Anyone keen to improve must train. For those pursuing world-class standards, training becomes a special study far beyond the scope of a slim manual on clip-and-go climbing. We can, however, look at the rudiments.

Training used to refer to strength exercises, period. The term now refers to almost any activity that can improve your climbing, including climbing. The first task is to determine—in broad terms—the physical and mental demands of generic clip-and-go climbing. Only then can you devise a training routine with results that will directly carry over to the cliff, not the basketball court or the gridiron.

LIMITING FACTOR

The fundamental requirements of sport climbing are technique, explosive strength, endurance, flexibility, sequence solving, and the slippery and altogether crucial mental game. The key element in devising a personal training routine is to understand that, without exception, *the most productive training will always focus on your limiting factors, your weaknesses.* Augmenting your strengths will improve your climbing very little. Targeting your weaknesses, however, conscientiously working at them and in time raising your defects to, or near, the level of your strengths, can transform a journeyman into a master.

First, conduct a thorough and honest appraisal of your climbing style. This is tricky work, and it helps to get feedback from partners. Ask: What happens when I get pumped? What am I usually doing when I fall? Would you describe my style as graceful, vigorous, limber, slow, pathetic? While it might be hard to determine precisely what is wrong with your style, knowing what you're doing right can tell your where *not* to concentrate. If power failure rarely happens, the field is narrowed. Having someone videotape you—with a simple home unit—is remarkably effective in illuminating flaws in your style.

Every climber develops a personal style based on exploiting strengths and evading weaknesses. Your deficiencies become most obvious when pushing your limits. At the crux, the excessively strong climber is apt to rely on raw power to the extent that he or she will even try to Rambo finesse and balance problems (making them far harder in the process). The weak but flexible climber will find himself—even on

Raw muscle may not be the first answer to greater success on the crag.

straightforward routes—contorted like a yogi. The climber with limited experience and technique will flail or hang out forever because he cannot decide what to do. The timid climber will move as slowly as molasses. If we could choose the most prized strength in sport climbing, it would always be technique, because with enough work, anyone can get in shape and improve flexibility, but technique is a much rarer animal.

Reflect on climbs that have spanked you, and try to imagine how things might have gone differently if your technique, explosive strength, endurance, flexibility, or mental approach were improved. If you're strong and flexible, but often fall off unexpectedly, drop down a grade, or even two grades, and

A slightly bolder approach is often rewarded, in this case with an easier clip.

spend six months or a year flashing as many routes as possible. You can develop brutal strength and Gumby-esque flexibility, but so long as your technique is flawed, you're still going to pitch off. Your focus must move to mileage on the rock. Weak? Work on building strength and bouldering. Stiff as rebar? Begin a stretching program. Burn out too fast? Tailor workouts around endurance, and so on. And don't get drawn into the "lighter is better" syndrome. Once you reduce your body fat to a very low percentage, losing even more weight will have negative effects on your endurance. Look at boxing, and the fighter who is always struggling to "make weight"—sweating off those last few pounds in a sauna, and so forth. By the eighth round—if he makes it that far—he can barely keep his gloves up. Diet, certainly, but this business about living off supplements instead of nutritious vittles is hogwash, and is a practice unheard of in virtually any other sport. Listen to your body. Eat sensibly, stay lean, climb hard.

Many superb new training routines, described in magazines and books, address every conceivable weakness a climber might have. Read up, and have at it. And be patient. A climber who cannot touch his toes should not expect to perform the splits in a week. But maybe in a year . . .

POWER AND MIND

As you draw closer and closer to the technical ceiling, the limiting physical factor commonly comes down to explosive strength. A world-class climber will have extraordinary endurance because he (or she) climbs so much. Having done tens of thousands of difficult moves, the climber's responses to various sequences will be automatic, or nearly so. His technique is polished, or he would never have gotten to ace status in the first instance. Granted, the best climbers always seem to have a certain mental edge over the rest of us. In fact, *the mental aspects of clip-and-go climbing cannot be overstated.* But understand that the mental game for sport climbing is qualitatively different than it is for committing and perilous adventure climbs. For sport routes, especially when pushing the limit, visualization and concentration play a decisive role; but these skills can be learned. On adventure routes, experience and desire can amplify a climber's knack for mastering difficult technical climbing when real risks are involved—provided a person has special nerves to begin with. The fact is, courage is a gift certain people are born with. It is both a blessing and a curse, and has led countless climbers to their graves. In any event, clip-and-go climbing has never been and never will be a game of "do or die," and when climbers fail on leading-edge test pieces, it's often because they lacked either the mental tools, or that little bit of extra crank that could have seen them through. Because the physical side is more tangible, top climbers are always trying to gain that last few pounds of torque that will pull them over the top of the heap; and this is a very difficult affair indeed.

HIGHER POWER

Raw, flat-out cranking strength is a matter of explosive power, the kind used on the boulders. (There is not a single top-flight clip-and-go climber who is not a phenom on the boulders.) When trying to increase explosive power, a top climber is up against two solid obstacles: first, he is already close to his physiological limit; and second, he is fighting against his own genetic make-up. Natural tendon size and strength, and the manner and location in which they are attached to the bone, directly influences a person's power. So does the triad of muscles, sinews and skeletal dimensions, and their relationship to each other. For instance, the cranes used to erect high rise buildings are often modified—fitted with bigger cables, the pulleys adjusted ever so slightly—with the effect that the crane's strength is dramatically increased. Unlike the crane, you cannot alter the physics of your sinews or bones, though you can increase tendon strength and connective tissues— with time. No less instrumental is the body's muscular make-up. Sprinters and explosive-strength athletes have a higher percentage of "fast-twitch" muscle fiber than the normal person. Though a person can, to some degree, convert "slow-twitch" fibers to fast-twitch ones, given the same training, the person with a genetically larger amount of high-twitch fibers will always have the explosive edge.

Whatever strength routine you follow (there are thousands), listen to your body. When working near or at your limit, serious injuries can occur, and minor tweaks are certain to occur. The key is to never overdo it. Once you're in shape, and the closer you get to your limit, the smaller the gains and the longer they are in coming. Intelligence, patience and close monitoring of your body become even more important than fiendish intensity during training. Optimize your training time, integrate it into your climbing routine and keep your learning curve as steep as possible by avoiding injury. Here are some considerations for training specifically for endurance and/or strength.

ENDURANCE TRAINING

General stamina is essential for climbing, but localized endurance in the climbing-specific muscles is the real goal. Endurance training on the rock means lots of climbing and hand-traversing on boulders (traverse the top lip if necessary), or at the base of the crags, especially on big holds. Spend too much time crimping on tweakers, and finger pain becomes the limiting factor. The all-out, forearms-feel-like-ironwood pump is the desired result of an endurance workout. Continuous, uninterrupted climbing is best. Once you begin hand-traversing as a routine, 30 minutes of continuous climbing is an attainable goal. Another effective practice is to rig a toprope over a route that is well within your range and climb it several times in succession, then change ends with your partner, and in turn, crank it several more times. No matter how pumped you get, always strive to climb fluidly and under control, just as you should with all aspects of training and climbing.

If you cannot draw an adequate pump on a vertical wall, resist the temptation to move onto smaller holds. Rather, jump onto a steeper wall where the holds are large but the pull of gravity is much more severe.

No matter the routine, always warm up thoroughly. Start on easy, lower-angled ground and gradually load the arms. Increase the angle as the sweat starts to run. Spend 10 to 15 minutes doing easy climbing and light stretching. Avoid the "flash pump" associated with starting off with hard cranking. The notion is to warm up the forearms, joints and tendons, not shock them. Establish a good warm-up routine and follow it every time.

STRENGTH TRAINING

Strength training on the rock comes through bouldering, and redpoints, including toprope rehearsals. Crank away on hard problems, with ample rests between burns, and even longer intervals between all-out efforts. Again, warm up, and strive to stay relaxed even when cranking through cruxes.

There are many popular cross-training routines that sport climbers follow to increase their explosive strength. Weight training is one. Whatever routine you settle upon, have the discipline to strive after long-term goals. Trying too much, too fast is the quickest way to get injured, necessitating a long lay-off, and defeats the entire purpose of training in the first place.

Suggested weekly training strategies:

OFF SEASON
Monday - technique/endurance
Tuesday - rest
Wednesday - strength
Thursday - rest
Friday - Technique/endurance
Saturday - cross-train or strength
Sunday - cross-train

ON SEASON
Monday - rest
Tuesday - strength
Wednesday - cross-train
Thursday - technique/endurance
Friday - rest
Saturday and Sunday - climb

LONG-TERM STRATEGY

In addition to a daily regimen of target training (warm up, endurance laps, and so on), formulate weekly and seasonal tactics. Go to a rock gym if time and location allow. Visits to the rock gym can increase your performance on the crags in leaps and bounds, and is one of the most common, if not the premiere, form of training for clip-and-go routes. A varied gym routine (see *Gym Climbing!*, also in the *How to Rock Climb!* series) alternating with cross-training (running, weights, or any other sport) and rest days is a certain way to improve. But without a strategy, you're much more likely to get injured, burned out, or both.

Let your training routine evolve with the seasons. For example, winter months are a good time to build a base of endurance; early spring workouts might emphasis strength and bouldering sessions. During the summer, maintain technique and finger strength between weekend cragging. Take the month of December off entirely.

DEALING WITH INJURY

The most common injuries sustained by clip-and-go climbers are not the result of falls or accidents, but rather tendon and muscle tweaks (in the fingers, shoulders and elbows) from overtraining or overcranking—often without being warmed up. Sport climbing puts tremendous strain on the connective tissues in your hands, arms and shoulders. As you slowly

INJURY PREVENTION

- DON'T OVERDO IT. Most injuries occur when climbers try to climb to their limit on every visit to the crag or gym. No climber can do so and last very long. Also, be aware of overtraining.

- REST. If you leave the gym or crag totally pumped, don't climb the next day. Any muscle pushed to to the point of failure or total exhaustion needs 48 hours to recover. Cross-train other muscle groups if you must train six days a week—but never seven.

- MAINTAIN A BALANCE. Work on your weaknesses, but try to blend specific strength training, say, into a somewhat balanced routine including flexibility exercises, endurance and technique drills, as well as some cross-training.

- PREEMPTIVE TAPING. Support fingers between joints with strips of tape (particularly crucial for bouldering/strength training). Once finished, remove the tape to increase blood flow.

- LET GO. If it feels like some piece of you is going to blow in the middle of a move, and a bolt is right there, let go. If you're toproping, are in a climbing gym or are low down on the boulders, drop off if you feel a sudden pang. Remember, most clip-and-go falls are benign, or less harmful than a ripped muscle or a tweaked tendon—but not always! Use common sense.

- AVOID EXTREME MOVES. Injuries commonly occur during extreme high-steps, dynos, reaches and lock-offs. Always strive to find the least taxing way to do a move or sequence.

- CLIMBING SHOULDN'T HURT. If a particular movement hurts, don't do it.

- CHECK HOLD QUALITY. Some handholds have sharp edges or cause the fingers to crimp unnaturally. Avoid them if possible.

- BE SENSITIVE TO WARNING SIGNS. Missing a day or two to heal a little tweak may prevent a more serious or chronic injury.

- ALWAYS warm up thoroughly.

round into shape, your muscle strength will increase quickly and significantly. However, the same strength gains in connective tissues take twice as long to cultivate; and if you're not careful, your newfound muscular strength will tear the still-developing tendons. Sooner or later, everyone sustains at least a minor muscle tweak. A few will come down with tendonitis, which may take them out of the action for years. The best way to avoid injury is to combine endurance climbing on big holds, strength-building through bouldering, technique exercises, cross-training and plenty of rest. Granted, always put the most emphasis on your particular weaknesses, but your routine

Sure, you can pull on mono pockets without splinting your fingers with tape, but do so at your own risk, as did James Dixon on the finger-wrenching Gunning for the Budda, 5.12a, at Cochiti Mesa, New Mexico.

should never become so lopsided and one-dimensional that other aspects of your climbing are neglected.

The best medicine for injuries is to avoid them in the first place. The information in the sidebox on the previous page may help you stay healthy.

INJURIES - WHAT TO DO

As mentioned, because of the high crank factor in clip-and-go climbing, debilitating injuries are commonplace. Aside from the normal muscle tweaks and strains inherent to all sports, sport climbers particularly are prone to shoulder, elbow and finger injuries, many of which evolve into some form of tendonitis. Having suffered these impairments on several occasions, I can assure you that ignoring the injury can result in pain so intense that raising or straightening an arm, or closing fingers, is virtually impossible—and climbing is out of the question. Concerning treatment for these conditions, I defer to climber/orthopedist Dr. Mark Robinson, who has conducted several studies involving climbing injuries. Says Dr. Robinson:

" Do the following to 'self-cure' tendonitis:

- Decrease activity until the pain is gone, and all swelling and tenderness disappears.
- Wait two weeks more.

- Start your return to climbing with easy strength exercises—using putty, gum, rubber squeezers—for two to three weeks.
- Do low-angled, big-hold climbing for one month.
- Move to high-angled, big-hold climbing for one month.
- Get back to full bore.

Anti-inflammatory medicines (aspirin, Motrin, Nuprin, Naprosyn, etc.) can be used to control symptoms and speed the recovery process. They should not be used to suppress pain and allow more use, since this eventually will lead to more problems and a longer recovery period."

Time and patience are the key ingredients to full recovery, and returning prematurely to high-stress climbing is as foolish as ignoring the injury in the first place. "The tissues of the musculoskeletal system are capable of remarkable feats of repair and restoration," Dr. Robinson assures us, "but these processes are slow." Furthermore, there is absolutely no proof that any treatment in legitimate medicine can accelerate these healing processes, save the use of anti-inflammatory drugs, which simply eliminate restrictions and allow natural healing to proceed. All the fancy gadgets and expensive therapy can't do a damn thing for tendon injuries. Understand that if you have good insurance, you probably will be referred to a sports medicine clinic. Such establishments are not in business to refuse your money, and 99 clinics out of a hundred will keep you coming back—so long as they can bilk your insurance. I've (J.L.) gone through the whole routine at a famous clinic, and after several months was no better off than if I'd simply purchased a bottle of generic ibuprofen (Motrin), and spent two months in the library reading Jet. In extreme or very specific cases, an injection of time-released cortisone can work wonders. But it also can do more damage than good. Each injury is a little different, and there is no generic verdict on the long-term effectiveness of cortisone. My father, a surgeon, told me that whenever you try to rush nature, you invariably run into problems. The safest bet is to go the conservative route, and simply wait out the injury.

Bouldering at Redstone,
Colorado.

MENTAL MUSCLE

With clip-and-go climbing, the mental game is in large part an exercise in letting go of psychological barriers. Preparatory to a climb close to, or at, your perceived limit, programming your mind with visual images of probable sequences is vital. Playing the programs in your mind *after* boot touches rock is to annul the benefit of the programming ritual and to impair your capacity to perform in a state of "no-mind," the crowning experience of climbing. I hear climbers often grumble about how complicated the whole business is. In fact, climbing is only complicated when you cast off with a head full of mental constructs, maxims, "films," fears, doubts—all the psychological dead weight a busy mind can muster. Work the route, certainly; but don't work your mind at the same time. Once you tie in, leave the rituals and worries behind. Virtually every practical mental ritual (applicable to climbing) aspires to place you in that calm ocean leagues beyond wanting and fretting, past mantras, visualizations, textbooks and experts, where the body is free to go about its work in a guileless, natural state. Renzai masters suggest that if during meditation you meet the Buddha, kill the Buddha. If you're crimping away on some dreadful test piece, and visualizations and notions about technique impose themselves, kill the "movies" and the notions and *just climb*. The moves might be hard, but we are suited for the work, spending as we do most of our waking hours moving our feet and hands and torsos about. A large part of our brain function is given to the task of physical movement, so let it work.

Our orientation directly affects our performance as well. Folks putting too much stake on a mere rock climb, who appraise the value of their very souls by their successes or failures, will never realize their potentials. They carry around too much mental baggage, are weighed down with delusions of greatness and the imagined urgency of scaling a piece of rock. Lighten the load—beter yet, dump it—and let the mojo roll. No matter how you mentally prepare for a wicked lead, the second you tie in is the second to climb and only climb. At the true edge of the possible, it almost seems that the harder you "try," the worse you do. Let yourself go. Don't be afraid to fail, and you probably won't. Most of all, enjoy.

Understand that as you near the top, the mental game is the whole of it. This is just a taste. For a thorough study, refer to Eric Hörst's *Flash Training*, also in the *How to Rock Climb!* series.

:CONCLUSION

The summit was the ultimate goal of the first mountaineers, and glaciers and snow slopes provided the most natural passage to the top. Following the first recorded alpine ascent, that of Mt. Aiguille, the rush was on, and major peaks were climbed in succession.

After the easier routes fell, subsequent mountaineers found that some rock climbing skills were necessary to open up new mountains, and they discovered lower cliffs and crags provided a perfect training ground to this end. Rock climbing slowly became less a side show of mountaineering, and eventually, a sport unto itself. Once the most obvious lines were bagged, variations, direct starts and super direct finishes were ascended—each more demanding until difficulty itself became the prime ambition. Reaching this last phase took more than a century, and culminated in the modern clip-and-go route, a genre of the "Sport of Kings" dedicated to gymnastic, explosive movement in a relatively controlled milieu.

And where lies the human limit? Time will render the verdict. But maybe not. Perhaps each successive epoch will produce a genius who will nudge standards a notch higher, into the measureless future. It is fascinating to wonder just where the whole business will lead. One thing is for sure: Climbing never stays still for very long, rarely for more than a generation. When the focus shifts back to adventure climbing, as it someday will, the technical skills developed on the clip-and-go circuit will spawn a species of climbing previously unthinkable.

And what will dance through the head of a future master, crimping on the merest wart, 60 feet out and 17 pitches up a granite wall that rears over his head like a great gray wave? He or she will reflect back to earlier days, breaking in on the clip-and-go circuit, when dreams were open-ended and unfulfilled. Only later would he move beyond the sun-washed crag and onto the Big Cliff, and only now, crimping that wart and looking at a 120-footer, will he realize that those early days of clipping and going were the best days after all.